Lots o

by Chuck Woods
illustrated by Linda Bittner

HOUGHTON MIFFLIN BOSTON

Printed in China

ISBN-13: 978-0-547-01747-1
ISBN-10: 0-547-01747-2

4 5 6 7 8 9 0940 15 14 13 12 11 10

My mom is my helper.
She helps me
put on my boots.

My grandmother
is my helper.
She helps me
get on the bus.

The bus driver
is a helper.
He drives the bus
and takes me to school.

The crossing guard
is a helper.
He helps me
cross the street.

My teacher is
my helper.
She helps me
take off my backpack.

She helps me
read my book.

My dad is my helper.
He helps me
pick up my room.

I am a helper, too.

I help my little brother!

Responding

TARGET SKILL **Main Idea and Details** What is the main idea of this book? What are the details? Make a word web.

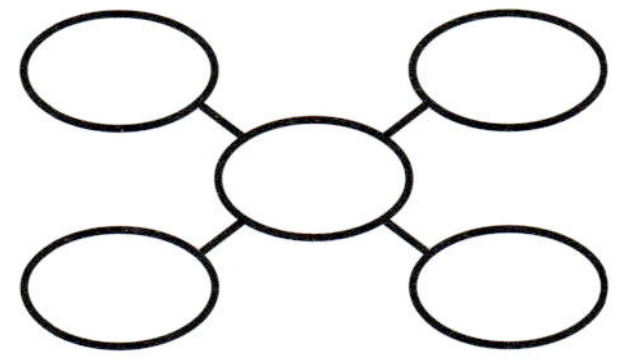

Write About It

Text to Self Draw a picture of someone who is a helper. Then write a sentence that tells what you learned about helpers from reading this book.

WORDS TO KNOW

off	**take**

LEARN MORE WORDS

guard	**helper**

TARGET SKILL **Main Idea and Details** Tell important ideas and details about a topic.

TARGET STRATEGY **Question** Ask questions about what you are reading.

GENRE **Informational text** gives facts about a topic.